AUDIO ACCESS INCLUD...

MW00817901

POPULAR SONGS FOR PIANO SOLO

14 STYLISH ARRANGEMENTS
BY EARL ROSE

PORTLAND MUSIC CO
(800) 876-9777
10075 SW Beav-Hills Hwy (503) 641-5691
531 SE MLK Blvd (503) 775-0800
12334 SE Division (503) 760-6881

To access audio visit:
www.halleonard.com/mylibrary

Enter Code
6680-0745-8072-4855

ISBN 978-1-4803-6468-4

HAL•LEONARD®
CORPORATION
7777 W. BLUEMOUND RD. P.O. BOX 13819 MILWAUKEE, WI 53213

Visit Hal Leonard Online at
www.halleonard.com

THOUGHTS FROM EARL ROSE

Creating the arrangements for this folio was a great pleasure. Ideas came from the various styles and musical vocabularies I use regularly in my performances; for example, "Empire State of Mind" begins in a kind of polytonal way, and "I Knew You Were Trouble." uses an Alberti bass figure throughout. Chord clusters introduce "My Valentine," and later, chords built on parallel fourths (which I also use in "The Scientist"). I truly believe each of these songs will be around for a long time because each one contains a strong melody accompanied by stimulating harmonies—signs of a "classic" piece of music.

My process in creating these arrangements was to first write them and, following that, to record them. In the recordings there are several instances where I spontaneously played something slightly different than what I had originally written—a variation on my original arrangement. I encourage you to do the same and, in the spirit of improvisation, use your own creativity to further develop my interpretations of these songs.

Hope you enjoy.

New York, New York
November 2014

With special thanks to Max Tuana i Guitart

CONTENTS

EMPIRE STATE OF MIND

Words and Music by ALICIA KEYS,
SHAWN CARTER, JANE'T SEWELL,
ANGELA HUNTE, AL SHUCKBURGH,
BERT KEYES and SYLVIA ROBINSON
Arranged by Earl Rose

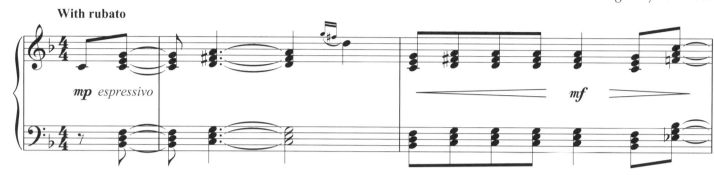

EXIT MUSIC
(For a Film)

Words and Music by THOMAS YORKE,
JONATHAN GREENWOOD, COLIN GREENWOOD,
EDWARD O'BRIEN and PHILIP SELWAY
Arranged by Earl Rose

With feeling

HAPPY
from DESPICABLE ME 2

Words and Music by
PHARRELL WILLIAMS
Arranged by Earl Rose

I KNEW YOU WERE TROUBLE.

Words and Music by TAYLOR SWIFT,
SHELLBACK and MAX MARTIN
Arranged by Earl Rose

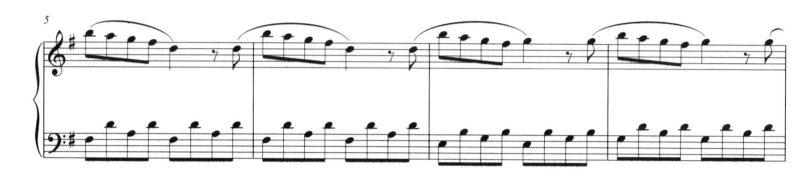

JUST GIVE ME A REASON

Words and Music by ALECIA MOORE,
JEFF BHASKER and NATE RUESS
Arranged by Earl Rose

LOVE THE WAY YOU LIE

Words and Music by ALEXANDER GRANT,
MARSHALL MATHERS and HOLLY HAFERMAN
Arranged by Earl Rose

D.S. al Coda

MY VALENTINE

Words and Music by
PAUL McCARTNEY
Arranged by Earl Rose

NEED YOU NOW

Words and Music by HILLARY SCOTT,
CHARLES KELLEY, DAVE HAYWOOD
and JOSH KEAR
Arranged by Earl Rose

RADIOACTIVE

Words and Music by DANIEL REYNOLDS,
BENJAMIN McKEE, DANIEL SERMON,
ALEXANDER GRANT and JOSH MOSSER
Arranged by Earl Rose

THE SCIENTIST

Words and Music by GUY BERRYMAN,
JON BUCKLAND, WILL CHAMPION
and CHRIS MARTIN
Arranged by Earl Rose

SKYFALL
from the Motion Picture SKYFALL

Words and Music by ADELE ADKINS
and PAUL EPWORTH
Arranged by Earl Rose

SOMEONE LIKE YOU

Words and Music by ADELE ADKINS
and DAN WILSON
Arranged by Earl Rose

UNCONDITIONALLY

Words and Music by KATY PERRY,
MAX MARTIN, LUKASZ GOTTWALD
and HENRY WALTER
Arranged by Earl Rose

Moderately

WHEN I WAS YOUR MAN

Words and Music by BRUNO MARS,
ARI LEVINE, PHILIP LAWRENCE
and ANDREW WYATT
Arranged by Earl Rose

ABOUT THE ARRANGER

PHOTO CREDIT: MARTA GUITART

Emmy Award-winning pianist/composer **EARL ROSE** has had wide-ranging success in motion pictures, television, and recording. His platinum-selling hit "Every Beat of My Heart" was co-written and recorded by Brian McKnight, and artists such as Olivia Newton-John, Johnny Mathis, and Peabo Bryson have recorded his music.

Earl's original film and television credits are prolific. They include the scores for the American Masters' PBS documentary *Johnny Carson: King of Late Night* and the Peabody-winning film *Inventing L.A.: The Chandlers and Their Times*. (He also recorded the original soundtracks to both films.) Earl appeared and performed in the film *New Year's Eve*, and has had his music featured in the television shows *Pan Am* and *Bored to Death*. He composed the scores for numerous History Channel documentaries, and his score for *Wake Island: Alamo of the Pacific* received an Emmy nomination. Earl's other television credits include *The Tonight Show Starring Johnny Carson*, *Captain Kangaroo*, and *All My Children*. His feature film credits also include original solo piano music in *White Oleander*, an acclaimed jazz-flavored score for *Mad Dog Time*, as well as music arrangements in *The Object of My Affection*.

Earl Rose lives in New York City and performs regularly in the United States and internationally.